Naming the Roses

KIM NORIEGA

POEMS

Naming the Roses
First Edition 2024 © Kim Noriega
All rights reserved

Published in the United States of America by
AIM Higher, Inc.
West Hurley, New York

ISBN
979-8-9863699-0-7 (Hardcover)
979-8-9863699-1-4 (Paperback)

LCCN
2024933361

Book design: Shanna Compton
Copy editor: Cindy Hochman of "100 Proof" Copyediting Services
Back cover poem: "Redbird" by Kim Noriega

Cover art: *Naming the Roses*, acrylic on board, © Sarah Luczaj, by kind
permission of the artist
Photograph: Nasim Luczaj

Ordering & Contact
do@aimhigher.org

Contents

Coda

Proem

The power of naming is at least two-fold: naming defines the quality and value of that which is named—and it also denies reality and value to that which is never named, never uttered. That which has no name, that for which we have no words or concepts, is rendered mute and invisible: powerless to inform or transform our consciousness or our experience, our understanding, our vision; powerless to claim its own existence.... This has been the situation of women in our world.

—B. Du Bois, as quoted in *Convicted Survivors: The Imprisonment of Battered Women Who Kill,* by Elizabeth Dermody Leonard

Name Me

Name me the girl
with the slate-blue eyes,
the girl who sits under the apple tree,
your apple-cheeked bride.

Name me your lover—

the mother of your eight-pound baby boy.

Name me *sugar lips.*
Name me *honey-girl.*
Name me *sweet potato pie.*

Name me the woman
with the black-and-blue eye.

Name me white roses.
Name me *I swear, baby.*

Name me crushed larynx.
Name me fractured mandible.
Name me *but I was high, baby;*
it don't count when you're high.

Name me *whore.*
Name me *get in that fuckin' kitchen,*
bitch.

Name me dislocated shoulder.
Name me *what ya gonna do,*
have me arrested?

Name me *I dare you*
to try and leave me.

Name me the woman
with seven broken toes.

Name me the *cunt*
you tell not to make
a sound.

Name me *tramp, slut, ugly*
ball and chain.

Name me the woman you love

to get up against the wall
and fuck with your .38.

Name me the woman
who found the dog
lying in a pool of blood
outside our daughter's door.

Name me the one who dug
the dog's grave; posted lost signs
the next day with our kids.

Name me the mother of children
who will never be safe.

Name me sleepless.
Name me *the little missus*
who bought a 9-millimeter.

Name me *shows no remorse,*
name me *guilty as charged.*

Name me not sorry.

Name me widow.
Name me the woman in cell C-15.

Name me free.

At the Edge of My Body

where my skin is / wait for me / I'm coming
    —Anna Swir, "Date," (trans. by Sarah Luczaj)

I.

Scalding
rain
pours
from
the
showerhead.

Transfixed,

I trace
the bloom
of my seared
thigh—

a rubescent
rosebud.

II.

Listen,

you can crawl
into the cave
of yourself,

abide there numb,
incapable of speech,

but see how
the cave walls bloom
with luminous mosses

how they gather
radiance
from the faintest light.

III.

Last night
I dreamed
I journeyed
to the desert,
sweet water
in a bota bag
slung over my back

that the parched earth,
when I wetted it,
burst into flames,

into a burning sea
of red-violet wildflowers.

IV.

This morning
I awoke
with the memory
of floating
in my own womb,

of suckling
at my own full breast
in that sea of myself,

translucent as a jellyfish,
but human, nearly.

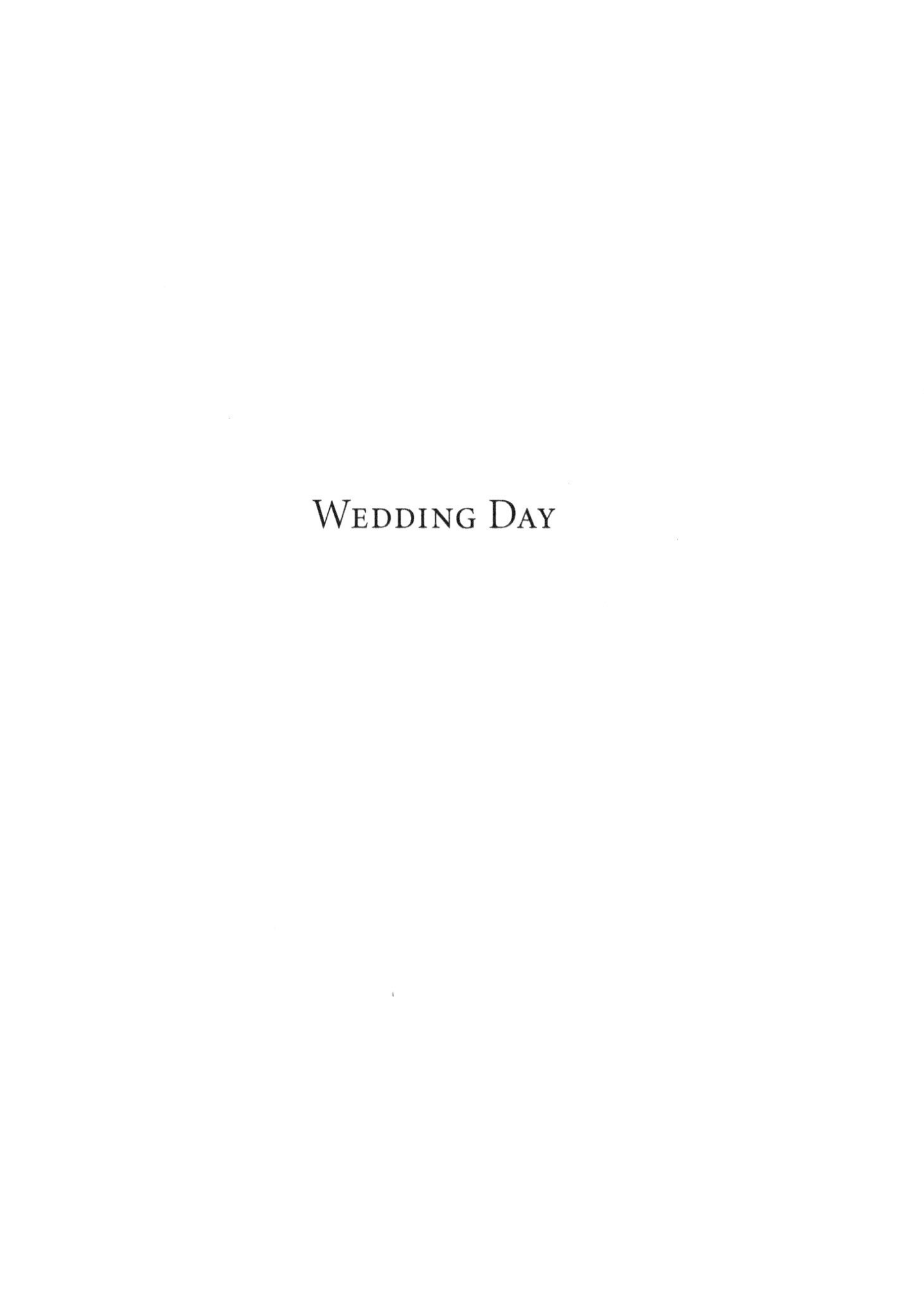

Wedding Day

1960, Just Married, Three Months Pregnant

Don't name me the blessing that saves you from being alone,
your lucky star, a sign of fate.

Oh no—
I am barely there, translucent
hands, arms, nose, eyes have seen
nothing
yet.

Not one word spoken.

Oh no—
This you will not lay at my barely formed feet.

In a Kirlian Photograph of Your Womb

Would I be revealed,
coronaed in light, tethered
to you by a ghostly, pulsing
cord? Dreaming, fetal. Still

swaddled in fear—immersed
in it, drinking it in, each twitch
of muscle drawing it deeper
into my cells—your fear

of life, of death, of snakes, of fire,
of mirrors, of truth, of silence,

of beauty,

of me?

BIRTHDAY GIRL

Heaven, 1963

It's my favorite photo—
captioned *Daddy and His Sweetheart.*
It's black and white.
It's before Pabst Blue Ribbon,
before his tongue became a knife
that made my mother bleed,
before he blackened my eye the time
he thought I meant to end my life.

He's standing in our yard on Porter Road
beneath the old chestnut tree.
He's wearing sunglasses,
a light cotton shirt,
and a dreamy expression.

He's twenty-seven.
I'm two.
My hair, still baby curls,
is being tossed by a gentle breeze.
I'm fast asleep in his arms.

Washing Dishes with My Mother

Even past my bedtime she'd let me
drag the red stool to the sink to help
her wash the dishes. She'd suds up
one side, then fill the other with clear

water for me—my job, to rinse and dry.
We'd scan the sky through the window
above the sink, searching for the first
star to wish upon, then the Big and
Little Dippers.

God, she was a movie star in the glow
from the overhead light, head thrown back,
laughing at my quips, hair—soft blond—
waving down her face, all Veronica Lake.

She didn't bother with an apron, or with
rubber gloves to protect her elegant hands.

She was so young.
Could not yet imagine
regret.

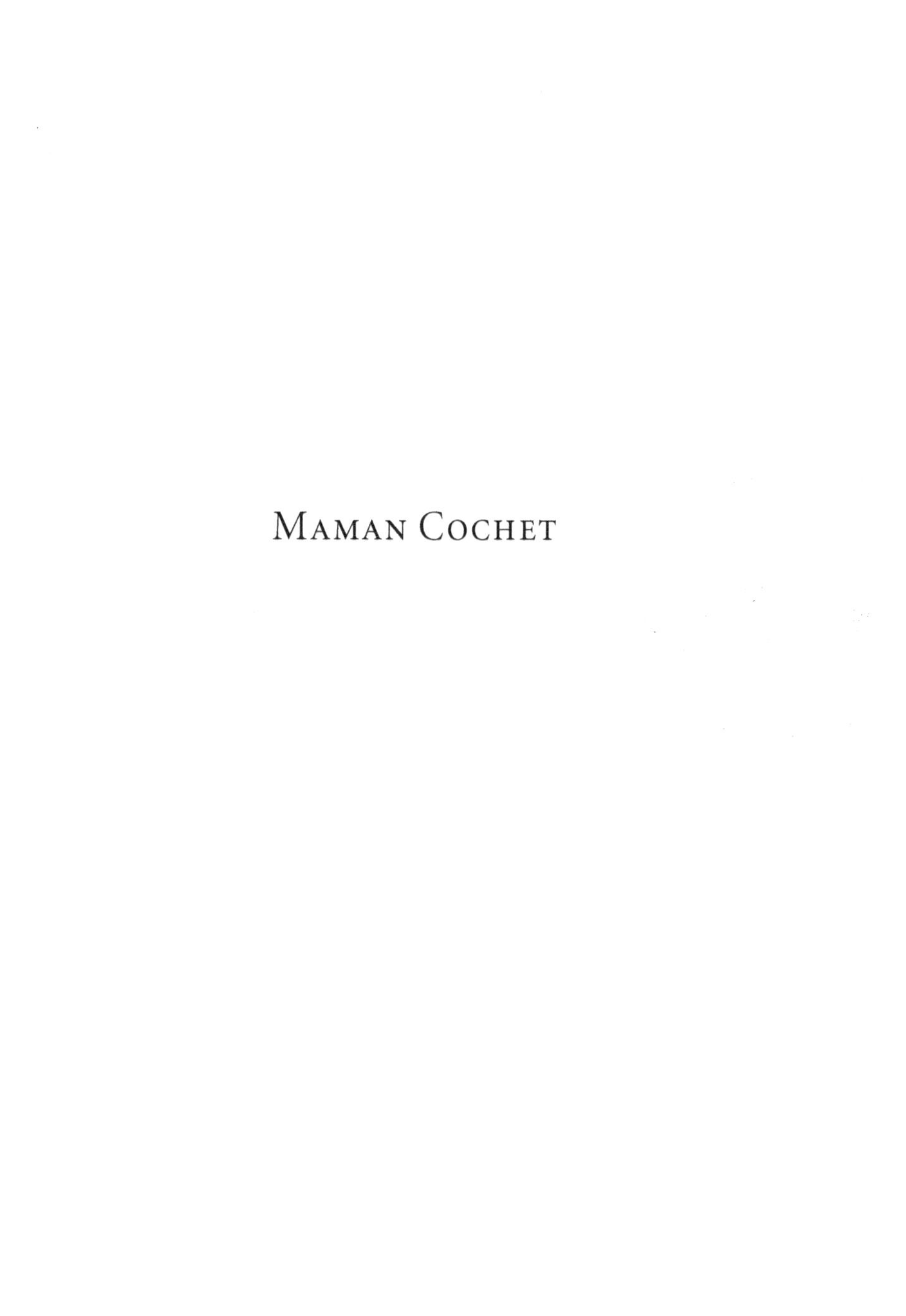

Maman Cochet

THE DOLLS' TEA PARTY, SPRING 1940

Two dolls blink at a one-eyed bear who sits
crisscross from your beloved collie, Patty,
whose nose forever sniffs the air above
a plate filled with Grandma's homemade
windmill cookies. And you—a life-sized
doll with your porcelain skin, white ringlets
twirling down your four-year-old face.

This must be Grandma's cottage garden
on Walker Road, a block from the lake:
Dutch tulips, Sweet William, evening
primrose, wild violets. Lilac branches
bent with blooms. Fruit trees—newly
leafed—apple, cherry, plum, peach.

Grandma stands beside you, her Cyd
Charisse ankles glamorous, even in sturdy
waitress shoes. Behind you both, against
a clapboard shed, a shadow looms—
the photographer? Your father?

You're smiling, pouring tea from a miniature
Delftware pot into a matching cup painted
with dainty flowers—a rare keepsake I hold
now in my hand, raise in toast to this moment
of happiness

                              —eternal, fleeting.

No Stitch in Time

It started with a smallish
sore on her chin,
an abscess, the vet said.
I administered

the prescribed pink goo—
twice daily by mouth—
which she resigned herself to,
and a second bottle, with no effect.

By the time she was properly
diagnosed—*squamous
cell carcinoma*—there was little
hope, but I hoped nonetheless.

Took her to an oncologist,
tried chemotherapy and radiation,
which worked, briefly. And
with the irrational logic of the grief-

stricken mind, thought: *I'll keep
her indoors; won't let her bask
on the roof midday; will seek
a second opinion, sooner.*

Surgery could have saved
her at the earliest stage,
but the tumor had grown
internally, would require

too much tissue removed
for stitching back together.
The wound would never heal.
And this is the way of it between

you
and me,

Mother.

Dream?

But why would I dream such a thing, and in such detail? I can smell the hint of rosé on her breath, hear her pink plastic curlers clack as she turns to face me. Can see her chest heave, feel each staccato word strike my cheek: *You know nothing*, my mother says.

You have no idea what it's like to lie there—just a girl, in the dark of your room—ears straining to hear silence but hearing instead the heavy footfall of a man supposed to be your protector. Who tells you he's sorry as he climbs, again, into your bed, covers you both with the white counterpane, embroidered with delicate violets—

but I did.

RAINBOW'S END

Poem After Reading the Article
"Jumpers" in *The New Yorker*

1.

Jump! shouts the man from his blue
Toyota Camry to the woman perched
on the ledge midway across the Golden

Gate Bridge. The article says that if she
does it, if she flies from the rail and into
the blue, she'll regret it, instantly.

Some survivors report a sense
of clarity, a new perspective gleaned,
the moment they flew into the abyss.

One remembered with regret
that she'd forgotten to feed her cat.

2.

When the suicide count
approached 1,000, a local disc jockey
promised a case of Snapple
to the thousandth jumper's family.

Spectators cheered people on:
You can do it!

3.

Sometimes I imagine you there:
enveloped in clouds, poised for flight,
on a red steel beam just beyond
the pedestrian walkway. It would
have been so much more glamorous.

4.

I was seven the first time you *got sick*,
drew you a picture of a huge, smiling
sun in case your hospital room
didn't have a window. Made my dad
promise to take it to you.

My parents said you had *manic depression*,
a kind of sickness in your mind. Said
it was what made you sit rocking, wringing
your hands, on the davenport.
Said you needed *electroshock therapy*—
which I imagined was like walking
through an airport metal detector,
until 2001, when I saw *A Beautiful Mind*—

the man writhing on a padded bed, arms
straining against leather straps, body electrified,
convulsing.

5.

When you came home, we visited every Sunday.
Dad would sit with you in the TV room watching
Jackie Gleason, Lawrence Welk, talking
about the weather, the new Buicks—anything
that wouldn't upset you.

Grandma cooked—pork roast with browned
potatoes, stuffed cabbage, noodles with oleo,
pierogies, cucumbers in sour cream sprinkled
with paprika. Mom would even let me drink
grape soda with dinner.

6.

When you came home you couldn't remember *things*.
I remember *things*, Grandpa.

7.

Nights at your house on spring break, nights when
my parents couldn't find a sitter for New Year's Eve,
nights you'd come to my room after Grandma fell
asleep, nights you'd hold a crooked finger to your lips
when I stirred; whisper: *don't say a word*.

8.

I remember the cool sweetness of vanilla ice-
cream, at the kitchen table, afterward.

9.

I remember the time Grandma found you
sitting on the floor of your closet, shotgun barrel
in your mouth, a toe away from the pearly gates.

10.

I was sixteen when you finally succeeded,
on All Hallows' Eve, on suicide watch
in the psychiatric ward of Deaconess Hospital.

They'd taken your belt and your razor, made
you eat with a flimsy spoon. They underestimated
your desire.

11.

You'd tried to slit your wrists with a toothpaste
tube and on the edge of a plexiglass wall sconce,
before finding your deliverance in the shower.

12.

Sometimes I picture you perched
on the edge of a blue plastic chair,
winding the gray vinyl curtain
once, twice, thrice around
your neck.

Poem to My Ex: In the Presence of God, or Something

You'd been on a bender—
three days and nights—
drinking, riding that Harley.

I was sleeping in our makeshift
bedroom, a mattress on the floor
of our living room on West 52nd Street.

I woke at 2AM, sat bolt upright,
grabbed my .25 semiautomatic
from under the mattress, unloaded it,
hid the bullets in the flour canister
in the kitchen, went back to sleep.

You came home five minutes later
twisted on tequila and coke,
pulled the gun from beneath the mattress,
put the barrel in your mouth,
pulled the trigger.

Wide Awake

See whore, you're the kinda girl that I'd assault and rape
then figure why not try to make your pussy wider? Fuck you
with an umbrella, then open it up while that shit's inside ya.

—Eminem, "Stay Wide Awake"

Nearly one in five women in the United States has been raped
in her lifetime.

—The National Intimate Partner and Sexual
Violence Survey: 2010 Summary Report

Misogyny? Seriously?
You can't bleed
from a song.
It's a joke.
I'm pretending, to choke the bitch,
to slap that ho, to cut

her up. Shit, what's a little cut?
Nothing serious.
A little fist to her face? That chicken-headed bitch
deserved to bleed.
Oh god, I'm joking.
They're lyrics in a song.

A song
can't make a man cut
his wife's throat. What a joke.
Who'd take that seriously?
Who'd bleed
some bitch

in Central Park? Who'd rape some bitch
like in the song—

with an umbrella—while she bled
like rain? Who'd cut
her skull with a dull, *uh*, knife? Seriously,
who'd hack his wife into bite-sized pieces? I'm joking.

Can't you take a joke,
bitch?
You're such a fuckin' drag, so fuckin' serious.
It's funny—a funny little song.
Laugh when I cut
you, bitch.
Laugh when you bleed.

It's hilarious to be fucked with an ax, to be left bleeding
in the dirt, in the dark, a hip-hop joke—
if you're hip enough to get it. No one's cuttin'
up your best friend. No one's rapin' your little daughter—just some skanky bitch
in a (Grammy-winner's) song
no one takes seriously.

Shit, what's a little cut, a little (of your) blood
for the sake of art? Nothing serious. A joke.
Some dead bitch, in a song.

Viola d'Amore

A fretless instrument with six or seven playing strings, which are sounded by drawing a bow across them, and an equal number of sympathetic strings located below the main strings which are not played directly, but vibrate in sympathy with the notes played. The head of the instrument often occurs with blindfolded eyes, to represent love.

—Richard Fleischman, violist

I. Domestic Violins

I did that on purpose—
gave this section a cheeky title—
to get your attention.

II. Violets

He tells you it's *all your fault.*
You don't argue, tell yourself:
you just don't want to get him riled.

But secretly,
you believe him.

Your equilibrium's failing,
you fall, often
run into things
with your face.

Women—who don't
but who should know
better—sneer
as you walk by,

tell themselves they'd
leave his sorry ass;
hit him back; make him pay.

You dab cover-up
to the bloom around your left eye.

III. Violence

The story goes
that my grandmother
told her second husband:
If you ever hit me, never sleep.

Still, when her son
smashed *his* wife's
jaw with a single blow,
everyone (except my aunt Linda)
slept just fine.

After reconstructive surgery
and false teeth,
my aunt never wore mascara
or lipstick again.

IV. Violins

I'll never forget
the first time I told someone:
The walls in my kitchen
have holes the shape of my husband's fist.
The woman nodded, patted my cheek, said:

Better the walls than you, honey,
better the walls.

V. Viola

I know he turns to you
just when you think
he's finally drifted off,
strokes your bruised face
so tenderly, you think:
He could change—

until he moves his fingers
to your throat,
begins to squeeze,
whispers:
If I squeeze a little harder . . .
while little white stars
explode behind your eyelids.

VI. Viola d'Amore

Maybe you're reading this poem
at your desk, on your lunch break,
after you've called him to *check in.*

Maybe you're thinking about this poem
at the market—thinking
about those *little white exploding stars,*
thinking of his fingers squeezing your throat—
while you're choosing a nice cut of meat
to roast for dinner tonight with tender
baby carrots and sweet Vidalia onions.

Maybe you're thinking
about the holes
the size of your husband's fist
in your bedroom walls
while you're loading
groceries into the trunk of your car.

Maybe you're waiting at a red light
two blocks from home,
wondering how *I* know
what he whispers in your ear:

If I squeeze a little harder,
just a little harder . . .

Wherever you are—

I want to tell you:
If you leave him, you'll be protected.

I want to tell you:
He'll never find you.

I want to reassure you:
He'd never dream
of hurting the people you love
to get to you.

I want to lie to you.

I want to end this poem
with a choir of angels
singing a cappella:

Alleluia,
we can all be free.

But there is an angel
peering over my shoulder
as I write this,

and she is not singing.

BEAUTIFUL DREAMER

KNITTING LESSONS
for Mrs. Hogue

When I'd visit after school, you'd be clicking
away, sitting at your kitchen table—a Marlboro
Gold smoldering in the ashtray, your cat, Huntley,
curled in your lap, crisp white blouse tucked deftly
into a walking skirt. In winter, a handknit cardigan
too, draped over your shoulders.

When I asked you to teach me, you said, *of course, dear,*
and handed over your current work-in-progress. *Grasp
the needles, one in each hand, firmly but not too tightly,*
you said. *Hold the stitchwork loosely with your fingers.
Angle the needle tips slightly together. Glide the needle
beneath the yarn. Now wrap around, pull back through,
and you've made your first stitch.*

I came back the next day with fat wooden needles
scrounged from our attic, a meager skein of peach
yarn, and our lessons commenced in earnest. *Slip knot,
cast on, knit two, purl one,* you taught in your kindly
Southern voice—that blanket of acceptance.

Even later, when I ran wild, stealing your cigarettes
(you must have known) and your son's heart (which,
surely, I broke), sneaking out with *that Miller boy,*
joyriding in your '66 Tempest.

Mistakes are to be expected, you'd say as you'd take
my little peach *scarf* into your hands and (overlooking
much, I imagine) peer at it over the tops of your glasses,
checking for inconsistent tension, uneven rows, stitches
dropped.

And worth fixing, you'd add with a wink, handing it back
—so there I'd sit, beside you, our heads wreathed
in a Marlboro Gold halo, knitting those same stitches
over and over, till I finally learned—which, I must admit,
took longer than I ever could have imagined.

What I Remember of that First Year Is the Snow

1.

We were sixteen
and the snow fell like stars
at our feet.

Do you remember

how we stole into the doorway of the church
to get out of the wind?

How your grandfather's homemade brandy
(stolen from his secret stash) glowed in the moonlight
in that jelly jar
you raised to my mouth?

I remember

how you persuaded me
to walk beneath a pine bough
heavy with snow,
swore *cross my heart*,

then pulled down that limb.

How we fell to the ground laughing.
How angels appeared in the snow
where we had lain.

I remember

muscles shifting beneath skin
when you finger-picked your guitar—

but I always thought that I'd see you again.

2.

I was sixteen
and the snow fell like stars
at my feet.

Before everything else—

motorcycles like dominoes
on our front lawn,
the drunken bodies of strangers
strewn across our living room floor,

the bar on 65th Street
where your buddy pawed
a local girl, whose brother,
the Marine, and his Marine friends,
beat you with a pool cue,
then kicked you so hard in the kidneys
you pissed blood for a month,

before Jack Daniel's,
Wild Turkey,
9-millimeters,
Speedballs,
Nembutals,
Black Beauties,

switchblades
to slit your wrists
when you came down too hard.

3.

I was sixteen,
and what does a young girl know of love?

What does anyone know of the open palm
her small world rests upon?

The hand poised
to turn that world upside down
and shake it,

to see the snow
falling like stars.

Do you remember

the church where we sheltered from the wind?

Your grandfather's brandy,
in a jelly jar, raised to my mouth
in the moonlight?

I will never forget that kiss
in the doorway of the church.

How you pulled me to you,
opening our coats,

snow swirling higher and higher,

your hand at the small of my back,
your teeth at my throat.

The Light of Day

1.

My daughter loves to hear
the tale of her father and I—
when we were still together,
just kids, really,
twenty-two and twenty-three—
out riding his Harley at two in the morning
past cornfields and meadows.

We were lightning; we were wildfire.

I don't know how he saw that pumpkin patch
as we blared by, but he doubled back
and chugged to a stop on the shoulder,
told me to *hop off and pick one,*
I said *no,* I wasn't a thief.
But he persisted—and I never could resist
him for long back then.

My daughter loves to hear that he had me
choose the biggest pumpkin, just for her.
How we thundered home,
my arms barely able to hold her giant prize.

How she and her daddy carved it together
the next day on the old green table in the kitchen—
gave it wild eyes and a silly smile
he let her draw with a fat black marker.

How they put a bright orange candle inside,
let it burn all night on the back porch.

2.

What I don't tell her is how my head
swam with fear all the way home.
He was drunk, but how drunk, too drunk again?
What was I doing riding down the highway at 90 miles an hour—
no foot pegs; legs wrapped around him; numb
fingers clinging to his leathers;
a huge stolen pumpkin on my lap?

Who would care for her if we made her an orphan
in an instant of asphalt and brains and pumpkin meat?

But I never uttered a word of this—
because the wind was in my hair,
because the moon shone on his shoulder,
because his hand was on my thigh,
because the scent of milk thistle was everywhere,

and the light of day was gaining on me.

Six Sonnets and a Tercet from
Beneath Seven Full Moons
for Dave

"Imagine" from Beneath the Full Long Nights Moon

I was freezing. I'd refused to trade my black leather
jacket for a coat that would cover my pregnant belly.
The gusts from Lake Erie were bitter. You held
out a candle to warm my hands by. That was the December
Mark David Chapman shot John Lennon. Despite the weather
we'd risked Route 2 in Bob's rusted-out shell
of a Volkswagen Beetle to get to the vigil
downtown on Public Square. In November,
Rich had left me—nineteen, unemployed, unwed,
and pregnant—for that bitch, Sandy, who looked
like Ursula Andress as Honey Ryder. I'd decided to keep
the baby. You helped me move to my parents', said
Rich *wasn't worth my spit*, painted my sister's old room
moonglow white and sweet Georgia peach.

"Rocket Man" from Beneath the Full Flower Moon

Do you remember May's perfume counter? *Lilacs in Bloom
Eau de Toilette*? I'd coax you within reach—
I swear, I promise—spray you till you'd reek,
then run like hell. You'd feign outrage, boom:
goddammit, Kim, and, laughing, give chase, dooming
yourself to years of such abuse. Or your role as Peter,
the goat herder, in the Butternut Ridge Theater
debut of *Heidi, Girl of the Alps*? When your two
goats (distracted by squirrels) charged off barking,
I nearly peed my pants laughing. You just played along.

Clear nights, I've imagined you, eye
pressed to your telescope aimed at the stars.
You wanted to be a rocket man—Neil Armstrong.
I wanted to be Emily Dickinson, or Harriet the Spy.

"Heartbreaker" from Beneath the Full Wolf Moon

I wanted to be Emily Dickinson, or Harriet the Spy,
till Richard Miller came back from Kentucky in eighth
grade; then all I wanted to be was Richard Miller's girl.

"Us and Them" from Beneath the Full Harvest Moon

Every Thursday, my dad hauled the trash
to the curb at precisely 4PM, which
is how I know the exact time that Rich
first put his lips to mine. You'd gone home to crash.
Rich walked me to my driveway, then brashly
took my face into his hands and French-kissed
me, right in front of God, and my dad, who flinched,
then, without a word, lined the cans
up on the curb and walked back to the house.
I felt the world go tilt. Then Rich kissed
me again and the equation of our friendship
grew complicated. There was the three of us.
There was you and Rich. There was you and me.
There was that kiss. There was me and Rich.

"Shine On You Crazy Diamond" from Beneath the Full Strawberry Moon

Rich was a lit match looking for gasoline,
of which there was plenty in Cleveland in the late
'70s. He wasn't on the spoon yet, but he ate
LSD like candy. Jim Beam boilermakers and 714s—
his favorite breakfast. He'd managed to stay clean
in military school, where he'd spent tenth grade
at the City of Olmsted's *request* that he leave the state—
or go to Juvenile Hall—for possessing and dealing PCP.
His transformation? Miraculous. Straight A's,
climbing rank. His parents were ecstatic. *Banishment,*
he'd said, was *just what the doctor ordered—a second chance.*
How could I have known those were the last bright days?
You and I visited on family weekends—savoring, not innocence,
but that costly freedom—the bliss of ignorance.

"Time/Eclipse" from Beneath the Full Pink Moon, West 52nd & Franklin

Rich hardly drew a sober breath, couldn't keep a job. I kept my
(loaded) .25 stashed beneath the front seat when I drove home
after late-night shifts as an upscale pizza slinger. My folks
watched the baby. (I picked her up on days off.) Those were *dark side
of the moon* years. Still, I believed the proverbial light
at tunnel's end was right around the corner. We had no phone,
which made my promise to never again call you in tears not (so)
hard to keep. But sometimes, listening to the crickets' night
song, sitting on the porch with Leiha, I'd wonder if somewhere,
listening to crickets too, you were gazing through your telescope,
thinking of a reckless girl you'd once called friend. Before I
took him back, you and I had talked about renting a house together,
with lots of trees, a big backyard, someplace to jump rope,
and out front—a smooth sidewalk where a little girl could ride a bike.

"Wish You Were Here" from Beneath the Full Snow Moon

When you told me, *No more tears on this shoulder at 4AM,*
I believed you. Vowed I'd never again bring my grief
to your door. How could I have foreseen
the distance this would bring between us? That decades
would pass before I'd see you again? Dave,
when I sent you my poems, I never dreamed
they'd cause you pain; could not conceive
of you not knowing about the *holes in my walls in the shape*
of his fists. You say you *should have known about those dark*
times. Say you *left when I'd needed you most—have regrets.*
I say, you befriended the sad-eyed girl that I was, came into my
life when I'd needed you most. You say *I'm your inspiration, a star.*
I say, make a wish on me, my dear old friend. The air is redolent
of lilacs in bloom, the moon is a sweet Georgia peach in the sky,

and I still refuse to give up my black leather jacket.

WIND ROSE

No Blackened Eye

No little arm
wrenched from its socket,
no bruise to hide
beneath puffy cotton sleeves,
no falling down stairs,
nor out of trees.

No special touches
(our secret to keep).

No pinches, no punches,
no pushes, no shoves.

No.

Each time he came *(Bad
Barnaby, thief of naughty
girls' mommies)*, you hid
in the attic, while I ran
from room to room,
calling your name.

MERMAID

The wind didn't still. The birds didn't hush. The lilies didn't
turn their heads. The mother's minted lemonade didn't spill
to the deck in a sparkling cascade.

I saw her little body sink, her chubby fingers flutter
like tentacles of a miniature pink anemone, a few wisps
of strawberry hair waving:

Goodbye, goodbye.

It took seconds. I slid into the water, scooped her up and out
of the pool to her now-frantic mother's arms. I was nine
years old. Afterward, despite the sun's warmth, I sat shivering

at the edge. The way her eyes had looked—wide open, beckoning.
Two sapphire oceans I could have seamlessly slipped into

                —stayed a mermaid there, forever.

STARDUST

I still have the photo of her, a yearling, all gangly legs and wobbly knees, red splotches from wild strawberries dotting her muzzle.

I was sixteen—still half wild myself—when my parents let me buy her with the money I'd inherited when my grandfather killed himself.

By the time my filly was two, her chocolate-milk-colored coat had shed out, replaced with an alabaster so lustrous I named her *Stardust*—the stuff we are all supposedly made of. She looked like a comet when she lit out across the pasture—a fury of limbs—tail straight out, streaking across the twilight.

My boyfriend's father helped me break her with the same Southern Comfort voice he'd used to woo me back for his son when I'd found him in bed with my best friend—*just some wild oats, sugar, he really loves you.* The same light hand on the rein he believed, till the day he died, could tame his son—*you know he doesn't mean what he says when he's drunk, honey.*

We broke her gently. First, he showed me how to get her used to the lunge line, eased her around the paddock, *walk, trot, canter, easy girl, that's right.* Got her used to the bridle, slowly; let her worry the bit; let the reins hang loosely across her withers.

After weeks in the paddock, we readied her to be ridden, rubbed the saddle blanket on her hindquarters to scent it, let her ease up to the saddle, shy, eyes wide, nostrils flaring, *nudge, snort, sniff,* then *easy girl,* slid the saddle onto her back. Let the girth hang unfastened awhile, cinched it slowly. Added sandbags, one at a time, till she was used to bearing the weight of a rider.

One evening toward the end of that summer, I hoisted myself up into the saddle and she didn't balk. Squeezed her flanks lightly with my knees and she moved forward at a walk; squeezed a little harder and she slid effortlessly into a trot. My boyfriend's father clapped his hands, smiled at what we'd done. Stroking her mane, I cooed, *Good girl. Good girl.*

Then I gave that horse her head. Leaned my body low to hers as she moved out in a canter. As she accelerated to a full gallop, I wrapped my arms around her neck and I felt something blaze up in her then—a sun-flare of desire, some ancient spark of inextinguishable wildness.

I could feel the heat of it burning both of us as we flamed across the open field.

Sacrifice

I was something, maybe,
you didn't want
to lose; something, maybe,
you thought you never
would. All those nights,

while the birds sang
in the sycamore trees
beside our window;
while we whispered beneath
the covers in your twin bed—

brother to sister,
lover to lover.

You said,
This bone in my thigh,
is it not your bone?

This blood, cooling in my veins,
has it not been
the pulse at your throat?

I was someone, maybe,
you thought you could afford
to lose; someone, maybe,
you didn't want
to love—

but love, my love—

I remember that last night,
how you fell,
how you split yourself in two
on the jagged edge of desire,

how I burned, willingly,
in your crucible's cold blue flame,
how I let you fill your needle
with the milk of me.

Wolf Moon (Lycanthropy)

I.

My hands shimmered on the wheel
as I drove down Old Route 82—
beneath an opal on fire,
beside a field of diamond dust.

II.

I drove down the old route,
past the house where we'd lived,
for one last look—the fields
powdered with virgin snow
and, just beyond, the forest
where we'd walked on moonless nights.

III.

A last glimpse,
because I'd loved you
there in the forest of sugar
maples and slim white birch.

IV.

I'd loved you,
but always came
the moonrise.

V.

At the edge of the field,
beside the road,
a wolf, pacing me, cantered—
all power and grace.

Then I hit black ice.

VI.

The wolf slowed.
I whirled in swift, perfect arcs,
my tires finding no purchase on the ice;
the world a blur of black and white.

Those amber eyes.

A hush.

The crush of metal and bone.

VII.

Could I have been a wolf?

VIII.

Beneath an opal on fire,
in a field of diamond dust,
it was your muzzle
heavy in my lap,

my hands shimmering
with your blood.

Notre-Dame de Paris, Spring 2010
for Doreen

God, Dor, this could be Saint Richard's *à la*
1974. We'd have slipped in (late) to Saturday
Mass, so that afterward we could go ice skating
or out riding bikes (ever so casually) past certain
boys' houses—and so your mom would let you

spend the night. In the last pew, you'd be laughing,
shoving me back into my seat (since I'm not Catholic)
to keep me from getting in line with you for Holy
Communion. The perfume here, of course, is less Avon
toilet water, more Chanel parfum, and I don't

think the French use Lemon Pledge to polish their pews,
but I can hear you beside me hissing: *Stop, just stop,*
when I'd make the sign of the cross as if waving a magic
wand, solemnly chanting *Abracadabra.*
Secretly, I loved the hymns, the voices lifted in song,
the *Holy, holy, holy,* the *Peace be with you. And also with you.*

As for God, I had my doubts.

What about Vietnam? What about nuclear weapons?
What about Wendy West stealing my boyfriend?

But you? You believed.

I've arrived toward the end of the 6:15 Mass, have lit
a votive in the Chapel of the Virgin with Child, and here I sit—
in the last pew—thinking of you, watching a procession
of hungry fledglings lift their mouths to the priest, who intones

corps du Christ, placing a wafer on each eager tongue, then waves
his hand and a cross appears—as if by magic.

My head tilts reflexively toward each benediction, seeking
some small communion with those two young girls.

Jesus, Dor, what would you say to me now? Another endless war,
138 gallons of oil spilling into the Gulf of Mexico every minute?

Your baby girl, alive for but an hour, in your arms?

Postcard to My Sister from the Rue de Turenne, Paris, 2006

Gray again and I feel I could do anything today; gray takes the edge off,
softens the world, makes me feel invisible, invincible, on this bench beneath
a canopy of old poplars, eating pain au chocolat, shooing sooty pigeons
from my feet. A miniature street park, so Parisian: wide boulevard, wrought-
iron bench, statue—this one a bronze of *Turenne Enfant*—and trees, the trees
I know by heart: buckeye, maple, poplar—

        and apple. Our apple trees in the spring,

opalescent showers, cave of green we crawled into, our refuge, me
with that leatherette accountant's journal, even then a fountain pen.
You, fearless, freed those brief hours from our mother's perpetual
scrutiny, graceful arabesque on the tire swing.

        A young woman

has just ridden by on a bicycle; long brown hair, silk scarf, pedals tucked in the arches
of black stilettos—

        oh Dawn, for a moment, I thought it was you.

Our guide, Mustafa, who says his English name is *Rick*, tells us this inlet of the Bosphorus
is called the *Golden Horn*, due to the gilt quality of its water at sunset. Legend says the gleam
comes from treasure, cast into the estuary by the Byzantines during the Ottoman conquest.

I turn, look in the direction he's pointing as the sun's rays reach the water, set it ablaze
—molten gold, 24 karat, brilliant. And suddenly I remember the golden *cornicello*
you wore at the hollow just above your clavicle, an Italian amulet against the evil eye,
like the ubiquitous *nazar boncuğu* here.

When I found you two together, I cast *you* out of my life, and then, mistaking his remorse
for *red skies at night*, sailed off with him—into oblivion—for years.

And here I am, sipping çay on a ferry at sunset, crossing a gulf (I never dreamed I'd cross) fed
by currents that run deeper than I'd known—innocence lost, our mutual betrayal, love—and
like the harbor around me, I am inexplicably radiant, lit from within.

Dreaming of My Ex-Father-in-Law on the Anniversary of His Death

You and I were sitting in the cemetery on Butternut Ridge,
backs leaning up against your pink granite headstone, cups
of steaming coffee—sweet, with evaporated milk—smoking
a couple of Marlboro Reds, Lena Horne crooning "Stormy
Weather" from somewhere overhead.

You're gone ten years and I've never said goodbye. Never
thanked you for all those times you plucked frayed denim
from my bicycle chain when I was an insistent girl of fifteen.

I insisted on riding in those long, tattered jeans.
I insisted on having your son for my own.

Thank you, for fixing what you could when I came to you
                                        —my old red Schwinn.

HEIRLOOM

This Rock Is Not My Heart

It's a legacy,
blood deep,
a worry stone
I keep in my pocket;

it's the story
of a man,
sitting in a straight-legged chair

—rocking, rocking—

of electric shock,
of a brain on fire,
of my grandfather,

of a leap

of faith,

of my father,
of his blazing wit,
of trickster tales told by flashlight,

—rocking, rocking—

side by side on the porch swing,
my father,
his story,

the talisman
I keep in my veins,

his blood,
his legacy,

this rock,
my heart.

Like a child
into his
babka's featherbed,
boneless,
already dreaming
of the river,
of cool mud
between toes,
of flight.

Like a bright
coin down the well,
still gleaming
with the memory of light.

Like a star.
Like a wish.

Like a windfall
of plums,
like an October night,
like our first snow
that winter, too early.

Like an angel.
Like a stone.

Like Icarus
into Brueghel's sea,
quite unnoticed by most.

Like my grandfather,
from the chair's
hard edge,

only a noose
to break

his fall.

CONTEMPLATING SUICIDE
for Leiha

While the body
of my grandfather
swings
in the psychiatric unit
of Deaconess Hospital

Sitting in the cemetery
smoking
with Henry and Lucinda
sixteen and pregnant

again

Beneath the hunter's moon
9-millimeter
on his knee

With the dust of angels in his veins

As a lovers' pact

As a marriage vow

As a *little Russian game*
that Daddy likes to play

(click)

Hi, honey

(click)

Put Mommy on the phone

On my daughter's
nine-year-old face
cheeks wet
teeth clenched
knuckles white
jump rope pulled tight
around her throat

As a family tradition

As a whisper
through the phone line
sixteen years old
2,000 miles away
Mommy
I'm scared
I think I took all the pills

As a prayer

Pinkie swear

Stick a needle

As a promise

Cross my heart

The Sky, My Father

My father, my sky,
my father, my wishing star,
my father, my Orion's Belt,
my gibbous moon.

My father, my New York boy,
my stickball game in the street player,
my *Lone Ranger*, my *Shadow Knows*.

My father, my teenager in the back
of a 1940s Ford coupe.
My father, my skinny-tied hipster.
My titty-pink and (cover your ears)
cum-white car,
my *Lucky Strike*.

My father, my Army uniform,
my father, my drive all night
from Louisville to Cleveland,
my father, married six months
when I was born.

My father, my cradle.

My father, my house on Porter Road,
my father, my woods walker,
my apple for Cricket the horse.

My father, my Carpathian meadow.

My father, my swing set,
my tire swing,
my front porch
in a thunderstorm.

My father, my bedtime story—
my *Fluffy*, my *Faline*,
my *Dumbella*, my *Endora*,
my father, my *Kick-the-Can Prince*.

My father, my birthday cake
made of snow,
my father, my redbird hat,
my *Queen Kim robe*.

My father, my *Kimmer sandwich*,
my *Kabimmer*, my *Kabammer*,
my *Kimbalina Ballerina*.

My father, my marshmallows
roasted on a fork over the gas burner,
my chocolate caper accomplice,
my soapy-water-for-dinner prankster.

My father, my hot dogs on the griddle
at 2AM, my box of 128 crayons
when I had the mumps—
silver, gold, and electric blue.

My father, my cowboy coffee,
my jungle juice, my hot chocolate
with whipped cream.

My father, my milkshake in a beer stein.

My father, my *Gunsmoke,*
my *Star Trek,* my *Voyage*
to the Bottom of the Sea.

My father, my *Happy Days*
in the black Naugahyde recliner.

My father, my nut roll and coffee
Christmas mornings, my Alfred the Elf,
my Santa's cookies and milk—
only crumbs and a note—*Delicious!*

My father, my Easy-Bake Oven.
My father, my burnt-cookie eater.

My father, my big red tricycle,
my father, my purple two-wheeler,
my father, my *No, I'm still right*
behind you, honey, keep pedaling.

My father, my *Andrews' Animal Haven.*
My father, my *Yogi,*
my father, my *Sheba,*
my father, my *Smokey,*
my *Mustache,* my *Mario,*
my *Bridgette,* my *Harold.*
My father, taught them all
to beg at the table during dinner.

My father, home at exactly 4PM,
my father, *my lunch box goes right here,*
on the counter.

My father, my two-tone Rust-Oleum—
silver and black—Pinto,
painted with a brush,
my father, my light-switch repairman.

My father, my apple tree in the spring.
My father, my firefly in a jar.

My father, my Lake Erie perch fish-fry on Fridays
my father, my pierogi,
my father, my VFW Hall diner.

My father, my *Ohio State* sweatshirt.
My father, my patron saint of holey clothes.
My father, my olive-drab leisure suit.

My father, my champion
of graduating early,
my father, my *Oh Kimmer,*
you can't mix wine and beer,
my father, my name written
in cement in the driveway.

My father, my stroke survivor.
My father, my *All right, I promise*
you I'll never die, my father,
my a-little-tired-of-living-dad.

My father, my thick peasant hair.
My father, my snake-veined calf.
My father, my *Andrews' eyes.*

My father, my *me too* love.

DESCANT FOR THE PNEUMATIC ORGUINETTE

I'm going to build a box for my heart,
                    my fistful of dancing plasma,

of rosewood, or cherry, or manzanita burl,
                    my rucksack full of *la vie en rose*,

lined with satin and crushed velveteen,
                    my wineskin full of cheap cabernet,

a beautiful musical jewelry box,
                    my pocketful of pomegranate pearls,

polished with beeswax and sandalwood oil,
                    my hive full of punch-drunk honeybees.

I'm going to build a box for my heart,
                    my teacup full of mockingbird song,

of flamewood, or cedar, or ebony burl,
                    my satchel full of black-eyed Susans,

adorned with snakes carved of lavender jade,
                    my mouthful of venomous serpents' tongues,

a beautifully jeweled musical box,
                    my reticule full of ruby slippers,

lid hinged with fine golden chains,
                    my heart a dervish in the meadow,

a beautiful box,
    he loves me not,

a musical box,
    he loves me,

with a lock crafted of tempered steel,
    my heart a kite on the wind,

and one bright key.

Conjugation of a Kiss

I kiss.
He kisses.

I have,
he has,

                oh god, we have
                        kissed.

I am, he is,

                  we are kissing,

    with lemon blossoms in our hair,
    with the scent of lemons on our skin.

We'd been kissing beneath the lemon tree in bloom.

I kissed him goodnight.

                He kissed me *que sueñes con los angelitos.*

Would I, would he, would we   kiss

one thousand kisses   and one thousand more

                  moonlight still hot on our tongues?

PROCESSIONAL

I.

Paris is walking me—

like a lover, arm draped
across my too-stiff shoulders,

like a mother, walking
her child (distraught
with some colic or another)
back and forth—

while I am walking Paris.

II.

It's almost time, noon,
when the hands of the clock
come to pray:

Dearly beloved.

I'm walking—head high,
heart pounding—walking
toward the rose-strewn path.

You can't see me yet.

My father.
Whose daughter
I am.

Redbird

who loves to sing from the blue mountain spruce
who loves to sing to the sprouting grass moon
who needs to sing to the stars as they fade
who needs to sing to her heart as it blooms
qui aime chanter en français des fois
who always will sing to the eagle in flight
who always will sing to the gibbous frost moon
who sang monarch butterflies into the sky
who longs to sing to the wolves as they dream
who never will sing to the rope or the bullet

who sings for you still.

Saltspray Rose

Sometimes, I'd weave my hair into two thick braids spinning down my back,
Sometimes, I'd ride the Arabian mare, bareback, through the timothy,
Sometimes, from a flatbed truck, we'd pitch bales of hay up to the loft till after sunset,
Sometimes, after sunset, we'd eat grilled rainbow trout with our fingers by the fire,
Sometimes, his mother would fingerpick "Fire and Rain" on her acoustic guitar,
Sometimes, I'd smoke his mother's Benson & Hedges menthol cigarettes,
Sometimes, he'd steal her prescription Benzedrine from the medicine chest,
Sometimes, he'd wash a couple of bennies down with a pint of Wild Turkey,
Sometimes, we'd spy wild turkeys, eyeing us from the pasture's edge,
Sometimes, the eyes in the walls chased him around our bedroom till sunrise,
Once, he chased his father around the barn with a felling ax,
Sometimes, I slept in the barn on a thick bed of straw beneath a Mexican blanket,
Twice, I slept beneath the stars at the thicket's farthest edge with the Arabian mare,
Sometimes, I'd dream of wild Arabians galloping through the spray at some far sea's edge,
Often, I'd dream of a Yaqui warrior, riding bareback through a sea of waving timothy,
Always, he wore his hair in one long braid, weaving down his back.

The Reason for Red Lace

Remember when we lay together
behind the hillock in the meadow?
How the crimson poppies, intoxicated
by the mere proximity of our fervor,
swayed on their stems,
then abandoned their petals to the sky?

How we were the aubergine sky!
How we were the russet earth!

My love,

you are the reason
for red Spanish lace,
cupping my breasts,
teasing my waist,
cascading down
the aisle of my hips,

trail of rose petals
blossoming at my feet.

THE FIRST STRAWBERRY
for Ernie

I'd planted the seedlings close to the house so that once they bore fruit, I could pad barefoot to the little plot of soil, pick a few berries for the morning's cereal, or to dip in melted chocolate after dinner. When the first white buds appeared, I never guessed how eager I'd be to see the white-green berries turn cotton-candy pink, then the deep ruby of a hummingbird's throat.

I craved the taste of earth and sun, ached to give you some primal thing, something grown; if not in my womb, then at least by my tender care. When I offered you the first perfectly ripened fruit, your words—*I don't want it*—were snakes striking at me.

I knew I should eat the berry myself, let its sweetness salve the old wound—*I don't want you*—but could not. Threw it to the ground to rot.

Next morning, that strawberry appeared in the center of our breakfast table on one terra-cotta plate, sliced into two—nearly perfect—halves.

On Your First Day of Interferon Treatment
for Ernie

I.

I wanted to be in the cathedral, in one of her *petites
chapelles*, lighting a candle, at the exact moment
you pushed the first needle in,

or kneeling at the stone hem of *Sainte Jeanne d'Arc,*
face bathed in a kaleidoscope of light pouring
down from the great rose window, mighty sword

de l'archange Saint Michel at her side.
But when I arrived at the appointed hour,
Notre-Dame had closed for the day.

II.

So I wandered her gardens—comforted by a chorus
of birdsong—beneath a canopy of flowering chestnut
trees, the watchful eyes of gargoyles and kings.

Knelt and prayed beside two blooming lilac bushes,
censers, I hoped might carry my prayers. Gazed up
and up at her spire.

III.

Light sweeps the ceiling of my rented apartment
on the Quai aux Fleurs, like a Parisian aurora borealis
shining up from the bateaux-mouches on the Seine.

I lie on my back on the not-quite-long-enough
sofa, thinking about distance, about your insistence
that I not cancel my trip when they scheduled your first
treatment during the weeks I'd be away; about
how, seemingly overnight, Stage 1 became Stage 2,
became Stage 3, hepatitis.

IV.

What was I thinking, leaving you there to face this alone?

V.

I look out the window, see a single star winking,
wish: *Star light, star bright, first star I see,*

but the star, I realize, is only a prism of light,
caught in the arc of an oval-shaped crack
in the windowpane.

Feu à Volonté: Tir, Autel du Chat Mort,
1962, Niki de Saint Phalle

Performance Film, Centre Pompidou, Paris, 2009
& Lettre de Niki de Saint Phalle à Pontus Hultén

Crabgrass, a boot, the muzzle of a .22,

                                                 I shot

a red-haired woman striding through a dooryard,

three white crosses, four toy guns,
a vase filled with roses, *une petite Pietà,*
a steepled church, a clock, a knife,
a statue of the Virgin, a woman sighting a rifle,

                                    at canvases because shooting

a plastic snake, Lenin's
head, a dead cat hanging by its tail, a bat
in flight, a doll, a skull—

all white-
washed with
plaster of paris,

                                        allowed me to express
                                     the aggression that I felt;

a woman, a rifle,

                               I shot because I liked seeing

an explosion of crimson,

                              the canvas bleed and die;

a woman, a shot,

       to reach

an eruption of plaster,
white smoke,

     that magical

  black rain,

     ecstasy,

  a flurry of starlings.

Naming the Roses

I. Wedding Day

Petals tucked
(for luck)
in his pocket.

Bride-to-be, and me—
little *sea rose*—
secretly blooming
in the ocean of her belly.

II. Birthday Girl

Look at me—
naked   joy

no stone of grief
yet cast at my feet.

III. Maman Cochet

At the seaside,
we sipped rose hip tea
from melamine cups,
played *Ring-a-ring
o' roses*, fell
to tears, laughing.

IV. Rainbow's End

You said, *There was only one*
path for a woman like me.
Seventeen and pregnant—
dreams didn't matter.
Women didn't have choices.

V. Beautiful Dreamer

I've been thinking
even the shadow
of a rose brims with
rain and sunlight.

VI. Wind Rose

What was I looking for?
Winter moon, Irish lace,
eventide, maiden's blush
                    —you.

VII. Heirloom

Pruning Grandmother's
prize-winning canes,
I sliced my hand deeply—
and there you came,
bubbling up crimson,
in the center of my lifeline.

VIII. Saltspray Rose

Legends say this hardy rose
stowed away aboard a ship
that wrecked off the coast
of New Brunswick. Swept
by the incoming tide to shore,
she blooms there to this day
                    —wild as a weed.

GREEN DUVET WITH CHICKEN

(English translation on a menu in Kraków)

for Sarah

I.

Oat grass, waist-high, waves *good morning*
as I pass. Elm, apple, elderberry, plum—
whose language I speak fluently—
welcome me, which makes me feel utterly
at home in this country where the only
human words I know are *nie rozumiem*—
I don't understand, and *tak, tak*—yes,
yes to green as far as my eye can see,

Lorca green—*how I want you, green flesh
green hair*—a sea of green, dotted with poppies,
with sunflowers drowsing, clucking hens, a fat
brown cow, a woman in a red babushka raking hay
into a stack, a dreaming cat, a cradle of green, green
and green and green and sky and I cannot suppress
this green bursting forth in me, this green radiance—*desire.*

II.

I'm walking to the store to get coffee, bread.
Lou Reed is singing in my ear,

he's going out, to the dirty boulevard

the clouds are congregating darkly in the sky
and I've forgotten my umbrella but do not care,

for this is the source of my joy—
this rain, this water, this life, this green,

he's found a book on magic in a garbage can

I spread my wings to embrace the sky beneath
which my ancestors dreamed of me, the verdant
pasture, the smell of piss in the bus shelter I pass,

and fly, fly away from this dirty boulevard

and the cloud lets down its waterfall of green.

Coda

Postcard to My Younger Self Beneath the Apple Trees

I didn't know I loved your hair—loosed
from its braid—a golden dervish,
or your plump little back, or your laugh
like the crack of a whip, or the sound
of your voice like a bell on a cold, clear
night, or your eyes—those bright, sad
stars. I didn't know I loved your knees,
crisscrossed with scars from climbing up trees,
or your fat little legs—what good could those be?

I knew I loved apple blossoms raining down in spring;
I didn't know I'd love my face, shining back up at them.

ACKNOWLEDGMENTS

Gratitude and love for all manner of wondrous gifts of time & attention, encouragement & inspiration to mentors, family, and friends, especially:

Ernie & Leiha Noriega, Lissa Kiernan, Sarah Luczaj, Cecilia Woloch, Shanna Compton, Cindy Hochman, Nasim Luczaj, and AIM Higher's Board of Directors—Tina Barry, Joshua Davis & Maureen Alsop. Also to Elizabeth Iannaci, Danielle LoPresti, Adrianna Renée Velez, Stephanie Contreras, Camille Helland, Steve Andrews, Michelle Tsiakaros, Matthew Stewart, Ellen Bass, Natasha Trethewey, Terrance Hayes, Kim Addonizio, Ted Kooser, Brendan Constantine, Steve Ramirez, Ben Trigg, my students & mentees, and, of course, my kitties: Sundari, MJ, Benji, Rocky, Shadow & Bella Rose.

Grateful acknowledgment is made to the editors of the following publications in which these works or earlier versions of them previously appeared:

Arsenic Lobster Poetry Journal: "Sacrifice"
The Bastille: "The Hour of the Wolf"
Connecticut River Review: "Poem to My Ex: In the Presence of God, or Something"
Crossroads: La Vida Creativa en San Miguel de Allende: "Poem After Reading the Article 'Jumpers' in *The New Yorker*"
Damselfly Press: "Postcard to My Sister from the Rue de Turenne, Paris, 2006"
First Literary Review-East: "The Farm, State Route 82"
New Southerner: "The Light of Day"
New Southerner Literary Edition: "Knitting Lessons"
San Diego Poetry Annual: "The Dolls' Tea Party," "Dreaming of My Ex-Father-in-Law on the Anniversary of His Death," "The First Strawberry," "Notre-Dame de Paris, Spring 2010"
Split Lip Magazine: "Six Sonnets and a Tercet from Beneath Seven Full Moons," which appeared as "Wish You Were Here from Beneath Seven Full Moons"

Paris/Atlantic: "Name Me"

Parler Paris: "Processional"

Tattoo Highway: "1960, Just Married, Three Months Pregnant"

The Tishman Review: "Postcard to My Younger Self Beneath the Apple Trees"

Grateful acknowledgment is made to the editors of the Visible Poetry Project for featuring "Naming the Roses," a reverse visible poetry project poem written in response to Michelle Tsiakaros's existing film (untitled) at visiblepoetryproject.com/april2018series.

Grateful acknowledgment is made to the editors of *American Life in Poetry* (in print and online), *Poetry Daily,* and *The Poetry Foundation* for featuring "Heaven, 1963."

Heartfelt gratitude to Cecilia Woloch at Fortunate Daughter Press for publication of my chapbook *Name Me,* in which the following poems previously appeared: "1960, Just Married, Three Months Pregnant," "Heaven, 1963," "The Light of Day," "Name Me," "Poem to My Ex: In the Presence of God, or Something," "Postcard to My Sister from the Rue de Turenne, Paris, 2006," "The Sky, My Father," "Stardust," "Viola d'Amore," and "What I Remember of that First Year Is the Snow."

The following poems also appeared in anthologies and the editors are gratefully acknowledged: "Sacrifice" in *Arsenic Lobster Anthology* (Misty Publications); "Heaven, 1963" in *Discovering Arguments: An Introduction to Critical Thinking, Writing, and Style, 4th Edition* (Pearson); "Viola d'Amore" in *Don't Blame the Ugly Mug Anthology* (Tebot Bach); "The Light of Day" in *New Southerner Anthology 2008–2009* (New Southerner); "Name Me" and "Viola d'Amore" in *Veils, Shackles, and Halos: International Poetry on the Oppression and Empowerment of Women* (Kasva Press); "Mermaid" and "Name Me" in *1001 Nights: Twenty Years of Redondo Poets at Coffee Cartel 1998–2017* (Redondo Poets).

"Poem After Reading the Article 'Jumpers' in *The New Yorker*" was the winner of the San Miguel Literary Sala Flash Nonfiction Prize.

"Name Me" was a finalist for the Joy Harjo Prize from *Cutthroat, A Journal of the Arts.*

"Postcard to My Younger Self Beneath the Apple Trees" was a finalist for the Edna St. Vincent Millay Prize in Poetry from *The Tishman Review.*

"Knitting Lessons" was a semi-finalist for the James Baker Hall Memorial Prize in Poetry from *New Southerner.*

The film *Naming the Roses* was featured on Shondaland.com.

Author's Note

"71% of pet-owning women entering women's shelters reported that their batterer had injured, maimed, killed, or threatened family pets for revenge or to psychologically control victims. Currently, only 17% of domestic violence shelters accept pets. Between 25% and 40% of battered women are unable to escape abusive situations because they worry about what will happen to their pets should they leave." —National Coalition Against Domestic Violence

A portion of the author's proceeds from this book will be donated to Kathy's Legacy Foundation, a nonprofit serving children and pets impacted by domestic violence in San Diego County. Learn more at Kathyslegacy.org.

Kim Noriega is an award-winning poet, creative nonfiction writer, and teacher. She has won the San Miguel Literary Sala Flash Nonfiction Prize and has been a finalist for both the Edna St. Vincent Millay and Joy Harjo Poetry Prizes. Her poem "Heaven, 1963" was featured in former poet laureate Ted Kooser's syndicated column *American Life in Poetry*. She is the poetry editor of *The Poetry Distillery* and a teaching artist with The Poetry Barn. She is a certified facilitator of the creative regeneration process and an expert-consultant in family literacy through the Pacific Library Partnership. She lives in San Diego with her husband, Ernie, and six cats, five of whom were once feral. More at Kimnoriega.com.

A Little More About the Author (Unbio)
(as previously featured in *Split Lip Magazine*)

Kim Noriega's single best word for:

1. What you're avoiding: *Entropy*
2. What makes you laugh: *Kitties*
3. Your superstition: *Lycanthropy*
4. What embarrasses you: *Selfishness*
5. How you slept: *Insomnia*
6. Your sense of style: *Red*
7. The end of summer: *Hush*
8. What you want: *Radiance*

AIM Higher publishes books that blur boundaries, negate binaries, interrogate, confound, and delight. We endeavor to open portals into unmapped, magical dimensions, and hold deep respect for intuition and collaboration.

Also from Aim Higher

Lissa Kiernan   *The Whispering Wall*

COLOPHON

Naming the Roses is set in Minion 3 and Minion 3 Display. Minion is a contemporary type family created by Robert Slimbach and released by Adobe Originals. Minion is inspired by classical, old style typefaces of the late Renaissance, a period of elegant, beautiful, and highly readable type designs.

The cover artwork was created using intuitive painting, one of the four components of the creative regeneration process invented by the artist Sarah Luczaj, PhD. She describes this approach in her book *Creative Regeneration* (Wayward Publications, 2019):

> When you raise the brush or squirt the paint onto the paper and smear it with your fingers, you aren't paying any attention to yourself at all. You make the first mark on the page, and the rest follows, step by step, from there. Just ask that mark what needs to come next. Maybe the red needs some green. Maybe it needs to be blurred a bit. Or sharpened a bit. . . . Who knows? . . . It's a kind of bliss that reconnects you to the power that's everywhere just ready to be accessed. . . . From all the rivers running and all the birds building their nests, from simple resonance and refusal to separate. Refusal to separate yourself off from the natural way of being. This refusal regenerates—it can't do otherwise. For no apparent logical reason, the regeneration is both joyful and loveful. It is full of love.

To learn more about Sarah and intuitive painting visit sluczaj.com and terrealuma.com/creative-regeneration.